To Cheryl Dupont and the New Orleans Children's C
for the Crescent City Choral Festival 2002; with thanks for musi

Happy Land

Andrew Young (1807– 89)

BOB CHILCOTT

* Open-ended ties denote a slight *gliss.* into the following note.

Music setting by Stave Origination
Printed by Halstan & Co. Ltd., Amersham, Bucks., England

ISBN 0-19-343316-8

9 780193 433168